CW00434157

THE LANGUAGE
OF FLIGHT

The Language of Flight

Mike Jenkins

ISBN: 0-86381-889-7

Cover photo: Al Jones

First published in 2004 by
Gwasg Carreg Gwalch, 12 Iard yr Orsaf, Llanrwst,
Wales LL26 0EH
℡ 01492 642031   ▤ 01492 641502
✆ books@carreg-gwalch.co.uk   website: www.carreg-gwalch.co.uk

To Marie, Bethan, Ciaràn and Niamh,
with love

Contents

Picasso in Dinard

We saw him there on the promenade
drawing as his head bobbed
in the sea-pool of his sketch-pad.

We thought little then, arm in arm,
between the wars, my good woman
and I, a duet of conversation.

So much later, in books and papers,
he was everywhere: that 'Guernica'
they claimed mirrored torture.

Believe me, I've experienced war –
carry it with me in legs and lungs –
and those people resemble no-one.

As I recall we stopped a second,
Elin veering a giggle into a cough,
lines like marks on the sand.

I've since viewed them, tried
to understand those sculpted figures,
bone-bodies stripped of the human.

Elin once joined me bathing there,
stiffly arched as she tested the water.
Remembering, I think of 'The Racers'.

For years, that single breast breaking
like a wave over combed hair,
has returned with troubled desire.

What if he'd painted us in Dinard,
awkward yet smooth-pebbled creatures,
would we long to exist elsewhere?

Mustard gas

My grandad knew it,
stayed with him till he died:
mustard gas a harmless name
for the poisonous seeds
which grew with his smoking.

I was kept from his dying.
Kept downstairs playing
soldiers with his regimental stick,
feeding the plastic duck
of his inhaler on the shelf.

Then the screens refused.
I read and tried to envisage
those craggy people drowning
in floods of fumes:
a man-made disaster
which didn't make news.

I was kept from their horror:
fractured families with nowhere to go
except back to blinding air,
to the taste of death on the wind;
to memories he never told.

Note: In 1988, Saddam Hussein attacked and destroyed the Kurdish town of Halabja with chemical weapons. The media ignored it, as he was then supported by Thatcher's Government.

Reversing the years

Reverse the years to the boys' trek,
their thumbs trying to hook
onto the chrome-nosed traffic.

Renovate the factory in empty spaces,
its reek of burning carcasses,
its gluey air sticking to faces.

Magnify the white house, its scream
of a woman in torture-dream
never explained in morning's calm.

Storm back the floods with lakes
on Linton's streets, the boys on bikes
from the brow of field-path heights.

Make hollows in the barley fields
of lusty rolling, as clothing peels
and the taut flesh yields.

Curve the by-pass into the village,
chalk the pavement with love's lineage,
turn the footie-field to a stage.

Resurrect the young girl with wavy hair
on a sofa, going for bare,
Saturday snog-in, tongues' aware.

Reel those eager boys back,
dodging among hair-gripping bats,
mad matadors daring the cars' attack.

The beach, my son and the alltime Batman

We drape ourselves down
we are the same
as those posing we condemn
soaking up sunlight
not innocently but complacently
reading about it
as chemicals magnify the rays
we drive along we buy
the things that cannot burn.

My son has made his nest
in front of me I tell him
of the north and ice melting
the next flood the cities
are a ball the oceans
a bat above them
the hole above us widens
we will fall upwards
into the gap and together
drift into space.

The cities drown as the tide
hurries in and people quickly
busy their belongings he sees
the need to swim
but how can we learn
to swim in space?
there is no air the tanks
will surely drag us down.

That night he dreams catastrophe
the trees have lost their skin
they all drop to the ground
and roots break up
into pieces of a desert
but God the alltime Batman
comes to the rescue when
my son lifted to a cloud
rides to the sun
makes peace between
Water and Fire at last
so everything grows a beginning.

Wind-walking

Wind from the sea
stripping away skin-dust,
whistle in a cave
clarineting into waves.

Voiced and voiceless
cords open and close:
lips, teeth and palate
all in concert.

She balances across the ground,
stepping out the rhythm,
both hands upstretched
as words are found.

Dark pictures of dawn

After the climbing sun
has taken the orange moon,
we're in the garden full bloom
with alyssum, viola, petunia,
flowers like ensembles
and a hedgerow of wild roses
delicate pink as her skin.

She's never impatient here,
breathes deep a westerly breeze
which spells the faraway sea.
Beyond our stile, always something:
calves with price-tags clipped on,
pairs of magpies rhyme for joy,
a bull approaches and stares long,
Mountain Ponies breakfast on our offerings.

Especially, there's the fence's screen:
the dark pictures of dawn
the light-projection defines.
We are two shadows in one,
the sphere of her head
another planet, our hands
black notes on wood's grain.

Learning again

It's like learning all over again
that word I cannot say –
not that it's a riddle
or even a mystery,
not that it's a cliché –
it's just the impossibility
for a four-letter word
to contain, to suggest
what she keeps re-shaping –
purpose, need, energy,
no trinity could equate
with an emotion
where instinct and intellect
merge like two tributaries
and I am taken
downstream rapidly
(never standing on a bridge)
following the erosion, the debris –
she's in her basket
waiting to be found.

The language of flight

Your head's an upside-down nest
from which thoughts will leave
when they're feathered full.

Your skull's a bi-valve shell
opening and then closing
on a sea of womb-memories.

Your birth-marks are unique
red veins stitched in cloth
which will fade with tread.

Your eyes open on each day
totally amazed, blue mornings
are prophesies of the sky.

Your lips curl out smiles
which climb the walls
and suspend from our ceilings.

Your hands grasp everything:
they're crabs and we're sand,
they bury their impressions.

Your legs are jockey's,
as you ride the surface
of the world despite gravity.

Your feet still kick out
at the willing air
as if it would spring back.

Your toes can grip
and monkey objects,
extra fingers you should keep.

Your laughter is all birds
before light, your soundings
the language of flight.

Those incorrigible whys

She's seeking down and down
with those incorrigible whys,
our little diver of the tongue.

She never stops for which or when,
it's whys she wants in her bucket
like sand or shingle, pebbles or shells.

She's never satisfied when we pause
like an orchestral note unheard,
we're silent as a sea becalmed.

She swoops for answers like a cormorant,
she can see them swimming
while we are sailing on the surface.

She goes down deep to the coral,
to the living head of rock,
to the tunnels unmapped.

She always comes up for air:
our responses logged, our hands
steering her back to land.

Crescent

She's a book of sheets
you turn over each morning,

a song of the road
while you're strapped in.

She's a rhyme on your palm,
the *Bangor Boats* of bath-time,

a frame of clothing
to pull yourself standing.

She's an ear so attentive
and arms for the circling,

a voice repeated and reassuring
like a bed of down.

She's a praise-giver
a sleep-rocker and danger-warner,

her eyes will be there
to catch and gather.

She's a crescent of flesh
warming every night-time.

Golf-balls and tadpoles

Two decades on,
the stile all-but collapsing,
wild rose a line
to snag our skin.

Two decades on
a younger daughter,
another beginning:
Waun's wilderness beckoning.

Out the back, over the fence
towards the rope-swing
hanging from crooked oak,
its tyre stolen.

We find golf-balls
in reedy pits.
She throws them, chasing,
zig-zagging for white orbs.

Cold as any autumn
a wind which mourns
the Gulf Stream, forebodes
more bitter Junes.

We find a mudpie pond,
to her an eye for stones,
the tadpoles' black pupils
dead still or flickering.

Up on the forestry path
she greets the Mountain Pony
nose-to-nose 'He likes me!'
Fear, beyond the skyline.

Two decades on,
land precarious as ever:
black seam of geological map
their lake of oil.

We hop the many rills,
water and sinking a challenge.
To go with her, two decades on,
without the threat of plans.

Old paper stories

Her hair the colour of bracken,
of leaves turning late
this year, once again.

The old man in his frame
not sure of his sight,
regretting what might've been.

Her coat clean white
of snow just fallen,
she crouched among the reeds.

Outside, places he once trod,
now the diseases rode
his bones to the ground.

She teased, her dog out of sight,
hiding and calling, starting
like a hare upright.

He couldn't catch a leaf:
old paper stories blown in
scrumpled under his feet.

Between shade and light

Acorns drop on the garage roof,
darkbrown, over-ripe as heavy fruit:
clatter and roll of fairground stall
they fall on lawn, drive, crack underfeet
like shells, their insides nut-kernelled.
November sun, last one the branches hold.
The street's deserted except for wheelies
and one hopeful sniffing cat.
I'm glad to turn my back,
to walk up the mountain leaving
pneumatic thumps of road construction
and column-buildings like timetables,
siren sound of decision panic.
My watch is redundant.
The sun plays hide-n-seek
I avert my gaze, heather and pine
bathe the air, my heartbeat
the cows' steady chomp.
Below, remains of oak forests
like wild flowers nobody need pick.
From the top, the Cynon valley
has turned to hazy liquid,
another season, but a burnt-out Metro
mocks browning, its bonnet
agape with lockjaw, registration plate
is ashen gunpowder, skeletal seats
are waiting to be buried.
I turn around, move between shade and light,
the town ahead unavoidably bright.

Allotments

You wouldn't to go there
except
          a footpath   a bridleway

the by-pass slashes through nearby
avoiding the measures judiciously:
power-station opencast
close to the surface, sulphurous

and on its other flank
smooth pastures and stoney streams
suddenly give way
                              to a scree of slurry
jewelled and clinkered
winking and ashen,
remnant of the name.

It's an independent community,
as if ready for a disaster, unnamed,
the railway-carriage stables,
horse-boxes and stacked bales:
the Steppes come to Merthyr.
A scrum of houses,
squat as props
but throwing smoke high.
Allotments and sheds fenced,
barb and broken glass guarding
rows of peas, beans, cabbages, spuds.

In Russia, Baba Valya
grandmother and murderer
who knifed to protect her crop,
no roubles matter like
this firm currency of the earth,
no patriotic flag but white flowers
emblems of survival:
century-ago peasants or serfs
knew exactly what she killed for.

In Colliers Row, not yet blades and guns
nor those illegal allotments
hidden like dissenters' chapels.
It will come
                  say the corrugated walls –
it will come
                  says the padlocked gate
and watchdogs barking at every step.

Restless statues

Within the oaks are people
who once inhabited this land,
each one an individual.

One leans towards the prevailing wind
carrying a sack of coal,
one bows the way it blows
peering down to town
and beyond, to river's end.

One is straight-backed,
upright as a deacon despite
the boggy ground, the storms
of a lashing winter.
Another looks diseased,
its charred and gaping holes
are the marks of a plague.

There's one whose branches splay,
waving like some orator
who leads with growing words:
acorns around the mother tree,
yet every sapling perishes.

Occasionally I can see in a shape
both a fist and a brain,
how deeds and ideals
become one. Then, just along,
one stoops low to streams,
the weight of leaves and fruit
hunching and humbling.

Within the oaks are people
who once inhabited this land,
ivy doesn't choke their purpose:
each a statue, restless.

Fires and the Comet

We followed it the night before,
you almost veered off the road
searching its brilliant spray, facts
you had to hand switching thoughts
to ice and gas: its tail melting,
each particle a year and the dust
we leave behind, how much of it
is swept away; its size from here
to London. We drive towards it:
the illusion of seeing its movement.

Nothing except smoke and flames
consuming stars, moon and the comet
we'll never witness again.
Those firestarters, those prodigies
of emptiness behind the boards
must look proudly upon this:
trees, bracken and heather burning
white arches of the graveyard
blackened, as ashes are falling
on lawn memorials each the size
and shape of a classroom.

Robert Thompson Crawshay

To think, in that casket
could lie the secrets
of the large-slabbed gravestone,
the reason for GOD FORGIVE ME.

To think, when the will decrees
the documents will be jaundiced,
those answers decomposed
like his corpse under fencing.

The last in that dynasty of iron.
When I arrived, decades ago,
rumours still rattled about maids
he'd ravished, ridden with whip.

How more than myth told
of the waste-tip he'd ordered
to obscure the church, whose sight
had daily insulted his appetite.

The way he'd stood witness
to his own decline, once glorious
ironworks pale and cadaverous:
photos his desperate heirlooms.

To think, when that casket's opened,
too late for any judgement . . .
the paper brittle as ash,
the scrolls' empty eye-sockets.

The man who lost his voice

What was it?
                Had you wandered
too far from your home patch?
Too many hotel lobbies,
maids and waiters tipped and bowing?

Had your voice been grated
by trying to compete
with the noise of traffic?

You were once a teacher
but the chords had worn,
so you learnt to cope,
to survive the drone
of touring –
                every city-face
in duplicate,
                photocopy music.

What was it?
                You still possessed
a house in the mountains,
you still spoke
                in up-down intonations.

For all those grand intentions
you left us behind:
terraces trailing from sky,
the rough-tough estates spied
from planes –
                you wrote *worker-ants*,
but they could carry
your weight a hundred times.

Gulag Gurnos, Stalag Merthyr

Barbed wire staves
along the rim of the shops,
razor wire from the trenches:
a music played
by a screaming child nobody answers.

At the top of a pillar
are the red spikes
of a Medieval weapon.
Regeneration schemes happen
behind steel meshing
seen before on pubs, barracks
along the Falls.

Ranks of green lances
around schools and hospital.
Cameras spy with General's eyes
planning the next manoeuvre.

Like Saracens on past Belfast streets
the police wear metallic suits,
reflections of those rows
soon to be demolished:
Acacia, Cypress, Willow
wither with rust, will not grow.

Subways – cleared of glue-bags,
empty booze-cans, torn-up prescriptions –
are filled in, concreted over
as if they never existed.
'Over there!' point the bus-shelters,
naming and blaming their neighbours.

Down town writer

A skin once into grunge,
he shunned all his GCSE's
as mind-bogglingly boring,
Shakespeare a torture
worse than chemical formula.

He once gave me a story
about murdering his half-sister:
it was like Edgar Allan Poe
meets Stephen King
on a damp Sunday in Merthyr.
'I'm gunna be a writer!'

He was down town by Tesco's wall
where all the alkies go,
up-to-no-good-boyo:
'I'll come up-a school,
show yew what I wrote.'

And I thought, there isn't
a single scheme could train him,
there isn't a single job to fit
his dearth of qualifications
to that tomb full of inspirations.

Holm oak

The one true memory of Bethesda street
is our familiar, exotic friend
with its black olive-coloured trunk
and full head of green, even after
those fence-busting storms.

So unlike its Welsh cousins
with their prevailing bends,
it stands – a prouder statue
than any stone or metal tribute
to a town hero – belittling
the gales as nothing beside
its mistral tales. So much part
of our place, and yet so foreign.

Bethesda has gone

Where it used to be is a plaque,
colourful mosaic bearing the legend
'Bethesda Chapel', where Joseph Parry played,
not a sign of its second life.

Even the street's cut in half
by a ring road and the statue
of a town hero with brassy fists
tells of another way out.

But I recall those dramas
like *Blood and Bread*, the words
clear as prayers: how congregations
became audiences, the altar a stage.

In the vestry's dark room
prints would rise from the tomb
and a potter's wheel spun
the psalms of the unemployed.

Above, in the gods, many frames
were haloed, as every cause
from CND to Anti-Apartheid
preached its gospels below.

Bethesda had to be saved.
We were its disciples, against
the council's philistine force.
I sigh now, every time I pass.

The last cobbler

He is the last cobbler in town.
If you didn't know its sign
you'd miss the shop, a crack
in the wall which opens up
when you enter his den,
a corner left unturned.

This is not a museum,
though on his posters are Garbos
and his machines would make Chaplin
eat a bowl of spaghetti laces!
There's no sense of order, labelling:
shoe-styles piled in decades,
but he can winkle-pick them.

He stitches seams like a surgeon
with a deep wound, his bucket hat
and tweed jacket the central heating
in a shop whose black ceiling
is tall as an ocean liner.
The brick walls are heels
scuffed or smoothed, tread gone.

His face a grainy bag of memories,
mouth zips open, wallet a small tongue
to tell of Canada, of immigration,
his papers kept for a willing ear,
worth more than fivers, tenners.
'10 pence!' he says. I think in D's:
befuddled, I proffer loose change.

He's closing down by Christmas-time
the town's last cobbler,
grandson a Big Mac manager:
new soles the dead never came for.

Another drunken night

Another drunken night in Merthyr
meeting in the musty back-room
around a flower-pot, Special Branch *plant*
with a soil of old stub-ends:
colour of walls is encrusted spit,
the sawdust more like rust droppings.

Another drunken night in Merthyr
and we're on the march again,
the spy with dark glasses on
is an old fella who wants to know
when our quiz will begin:
one question – 'Is the revolution after closing time?' *

Another drunken night in Merthyr
and the punters all jabber
in wacky talk, half Martian
half Skull Attack, except it's lager
in one end out the other.
I nod sagely, agree to everything.

Another drunken night in Merthyr,
the cistern's in danger of collapsing,
women are a species unknown,
even the barmaid's disappeared
down the cellar. Underground creatures,
our small, glass hills so bare.

* *cp. Henry Livings & Alex Glasgow*
'When this pub closes the Revolution will begin'

On Bargoed Beach

On the beach at Bargoed
the sand isn't seamed with coaldust
but with layer after layer of print:
the cliffs of a Thousand Books,
the colours of strata denoting
sediments of fiction and fact.

On the beach at Bargoed
poets washed up like whales
must be tended and served
with brandy-lacking punch
and rapidly melting fingers:
the librarians in straw hats
and glasses, clutch children's verses.

On the beach at Bargoed
the sea has many different voices,
waves of accents which break
over the marram's stiff arms
and the dunes of lined seats.

On the beach at Bargoed
in the shade of evergreen
towers of videos and CD's,
you can view fish on computer screens,
pour water over the poets
before they shrivel and crack
under a skylight-sun so authentic.

Prayin f' green

Ey, God mun, lissen up
t' what I gotta say:
wen' t' the doctor's
sayz I gotta lump,
might not go away!

Maybe bard, maybe okay,
but wha ave I done
t' deserve it, eh?
I know I lied an urt,
know I sinned a bit,
but I never killed nobody,
never put myself
before my own famlee.

God mun, I tried didn I?
Done overtime till I
could ardly open my eyes,
t' buy em tidee books 'n' toys.
God mun, I done ower ouse up
summin lovely, my ands
signin ev'ry wall an ceilin.

Yew're the ol man I never ad
(mine never give a damn –
sorry 'bout-a language!).
I'm turnin t' yew now
f' my kids an missis
an, orright, I wanna be round
t' see Wales win-a Worl' Cup!

If yew got any clout at all
gimme a lump like a tip
that diggers cun scoop up,
cover over with a new skin,
so I become like ower Valley
in my prime o' green agen.

Ol Lizzie

'Dear ol Lizzie!' they sayz,
'the whool town loved er.
Ewsed t' be wife of-a Mayor.
Grand ol lady o' Merthyr!
Thin's she done in-a war –
practiclee won it from-a bunker.'

But I know different, see,
an I int bein at all bitchy.
I know she wuz neelly
an undred an three,
but my gran knew er.

In-a 30's she reckoned Itler
wern tha bard arfter all.
She ad er two neices put away
in an Ome, local papers
even sayd they woz dead
when she ad a bit o' power.

She never sayd nothin special,
jest smiled from too much gin.
She wuz so bloody swanky
she ad people in
to do er cleanin –
paid them buggerall.

'Dear ol Lizzie!' they sayz,
'wisht there woz more like er.'
Er fewnral wen' on f' dayz
ev'ryone sayin she wuz great
(all them ones oo never knew er!).
Ow come she spent mos' of er time
in er posh ouse in London?

Wise yet whisperin

It defnitlee wern er usband
oo called er summin rotten,
spected er t' come runnin
with is 'Sit!' an 'Lie down!'

It wern even er chil'ren
oo wandered too far from ome,
oo bothered with all-a nutters,
oo ignored advice she give em.

It wern er mam, livin alone
in an ouse more like a museum
to er jest-died usband –
oo she elped out ev'ry weekend.

It wern the church she attended,
ev'ry Sunday, reglar routine –
the preachin left er wonderin
if she woz livin a life o' sin.

It woz summin nobody could touch,
nobody could count in pounds,
she'd found both inside an out,
a wise yet whisperin sound.

She yeard it as the mountains
yer the rivers, as the sky
yers the rain, as the mother
yers her baby stirrin within.

Ow low cun yew get

I tol er the moany ol cow,
she says 'Cover it up now!'
andin me a 'lasterplast,
'What about em Injuns
with tha singer Sting?'
'Less of yewr lip!'
I says 'It's on my yer!'

Nex time it'll be my tongue,
let em try t' stop tha.
Know one boy got is nipple done,
Games teacher ad im in-a shower
'You'll rust you will, son!'
Wen' septic arfter rugby:
all-a canoodlin in-a scrum.

We gotta competition, Goj,
see ow low yew cun get,
is boy Mark ee reckons
is foreskin's bin pierced.
Like t' see the 'ead
oo'd deal with im,
though there's girls oo claim . . .

Mus' be plenty o' tribes
what do the same
an look at em teachers loaded
wi' jewlree fit fera Queen.
Theyr rewls 're rings
roun' my bleedin neck.

Desprut t' get on-a telly

I woz so desprut t' get on-a telly
I phoned 'Millionaire' thousands o' times,
lost a fortewn – it ud ave t' be renamed
'Ow T' Be Pooer' speshlee f' me!

I woz so desprut t' get on-a telly
I auditioned f' 'Pop Stars' an 'Pop Idols',
on'y t' be tol I woz-a wrong side o' 30
an face-warts didn elp a celebritee.

I woz so desprut t' get on-a telly
I ad ower ouse all lit up
like Blackpool for Christmas GMTV –
a fuse blew jest as-a camras turned up.

I woz so desprut t' get on-a telly
I wen in f' 'Big Brother',
on'y my IQ wuz over 40
an I could string a sentence t'gether.

I woz so desprut to get on-a telly
I even volunteered f' 'Weakest Link',
but soon as Anne Robinson insulted me
I panned er out, spent a night in clink!

I woz so desprut t' get on-a telly
I waved my passport f' 'Crimewatchers'
while robbin a bank, but-a film
ad run out on-a CCTV.

So desprut I even tried Cilla,
but my sweaty armpits, bard breath,
gobbin talk an farty arse
give me no chance as a 'Blind Date' contender.

So desprut I attacked ower neighbour
with a rake, arfta ee got on 'Nuts 'n' Bolts' –
I wuz famous too late, stuck in prison.
On-a news, they got my name wrong!

Dowlais peer

I carn stan' snobs like im!
Ee may come from Dowlais
but ee wan's t' call it 'Dow-lay'
like-a Frenchman oo lost is way.

Ee d' say we're commun,
thinks we're all so ordinree
an the way we do talk
got no int o' poetree.

Ee's there in is pink ouse
like it's made o' strawberry ice,
pronouncin with a twang
an sayin 'Oh, how nice!'

Ee looks down is nose
longer 'an the A470,
is eyes like buzzard's t' mice
an his Car-diff Suit Co.

'We'll have no language here!'
ee slags off is daughter an son,
they swear like a coupla piss-eads,
wind im up by callin im 'mun'.

I carn stan' snobs like im
with is elocutionree yers,
my brother-in-law, but is law
is like one passed by peers.

Child with no name

I ad it cut out,
cut out from inside me,
the child oo never
ad no name.

It woz jest I couldn cope,
I woz far too young,
the boy didn wanna know,
my mam ud throw me out.

They took it away
an burnt it up:
I see-a chimley t'day
igh as my guilt.

An the smell o' smoke
ull always follow me:
my crematorium baby,
ash-tray little one.

I ad a choice,
I made-a wrong one.
But, I coulda cracked,
ended up crazee 'n' droolin.

Mos days I see er
down town in a push-chair
or runnin, cryin, larfin:
I wanna lift an cwtch er.

My worse nightmare agen 'n' agen,
them weapons attackin my body,
men in masks, them outlaws
stealin my on'y possession.

I never chase em arfter,
I never tell no lawman.
I see my frens, theyr babies,
an wonder if I'm ewman.

Nobuddies

Booze on-a lines
an-a poverty wages,
no Ewnions allowed,
dousin ower rage.

Aulin office furniture
up 'n' down, in 'n' out:
brewses like badges
clothes soppin sweat.

Breaktime bongs
an lunchtime joints,
we're all fulltime nutters,
survival's the point.

Spraycans spittin
an swearin on tap,
a painted pukedom:
managers paid f' sittin.

Nightshift sleepworkers,
filin-cabinet coffins,
desktop tombstones
an phone-bells tollin.

Booze on-a lines,
it's-a way to Beyond,
the doors 're back t' front,
legs 're upside down.

Foreman thinks ee's Prescott,
bosses think theyer Blair:
but us, we're nobuddies
livin off-a scenty air.

The taxi-driver's tale

I woz bullied at school, see,
ginger air, specs, nothin going f' me.

It wuz all 'Ginger minge!' 'Dai Carrot!'
'Specky red!'. I really ated it.

Learned my lesson, done karate –
no messin now, I break legs.

This bloke ee done ower ouse . . .
Shane James . . . yeard of im? . . . on drugs.

Broad daylight goin through ower rooms
till my little boy disturbed im.

It im against the wall . . . blood ev'rywhere
from is face . . . 8 stitches arfter.

Cops, as ever, done absolutely nothin.
So I got a baseball bat t' ammer

some sense inta tha no-good druggie . . .
smashed is door in . . . 'bout t' kill im, see.

Cops arrived las' second, stopped me.
In court, thought I wuz goin down.

'Ee's dead!' I tol-a Judge,
'put me in-a same prison.'

'I can understand your reasoning.'
I woz gobsmacked, got off totelee.

Ee wen' down for five yers.
Come out las' week . . . I got frens . . .

an ee wuz found dirty as a turd,
mashed up . . . onest, it wern me.

Cops come round all-a same, enquirin –
though I ad an alibi,

down-a club doin-a karate.
Take my son with me orready,

is red air a flamin ragin fire –
six yer-ol face, with a six inch scar.

Singing the blues

1.   The Ayatollah

I'd say Big Mick was the inventor.
I recall the first time vividly:
Edgar Street and Away fervour,
brewed-up despite a team
who could never score on passion.

The rubbled space at the front
of a ramshackle stand was his arena,
cheered on by the fanzine crew,
Big Mick, a six foot skinhead
into the Redskins and ska,
danced the full length, a display
from crouch to spring to forehead-
slapping parody of the news pictures.

Khomeini, that arch-demon,
just as we were, Cardiff on the road,
dubbed Hooligans, with a capital 'Huh!'
The Ayatollah was born, became
our signature-chant, our crazed
tanked-up, bloodless version.

But now, success bought at a price,
with play to match our emotions,
the Ayatollah's been transformed
into a ritual, switched on, performed
in short, sharp jabbing motions
like the sign of a cross.
Big Mick's stomping exuberance
lost to a disembodied voice.

2. Jester of the PA

Ali Yassine!
Name itself, a delighted scream
at scoring: Kaairdiff man
and Cymro Cymraeg Muslim.

Done his 20 years
on the terracing
through wind, rain and Alan Durban.

Our voice from up high,
our bobbing microphone,
ranging over the Grange
latching onto the Canton,
his seagull-catching phrase
SUPPORT THE BOYZ
MAKE SOME NOISE!

Forgotten now how he helped
to make the Ayatollah routine,
as he spins Welsh discs
and jokes from his box
a jester above the stands.

Ali Yassine!
His wit and mockery
rhyming with *fanzine!*
He trains our chanting
and our rhythms run
from line to line with the team.

3.   Earnie's first

Wales 1 – Germany 0

We always knew –
                    the Zambian Welshman,
always knew he'd do it –
                    the skinny malink,
nippy as a whippet,
                    agile as a squirrel.

Afterwards, he couldn't describe how much . . .
clichés flowed like sweat,
but his goofy grin
                    kid out-of-shorts
and the tears
              as he walked
                          from prodding mike.

Always knew he could –
                    comic-book story
of my childhood –
                    one-nil! one-nil!
replayed over and over
                    in our video-heads.

Little Earnie, our fave-rave,
doing his somersault
                    before the Huge Names
could catch him up.

Little Earnie, stockier from weights,
but still our kid
                    in the yard,
beating the wall with tennis ball tricks.

4.   For every mousey sound

Cardiff 2 – Leeds 1

I'd suddenly go from a bass to a squeak
so the kids thought my balls had undropped
or I'd had the chop or was just a freak,
a secret Bee Gee's impersonator
come, at last, out of the closet.

But it was well worth it, for that yell
at Young's goal which lasted till the whistle,
a yell of sheer joy, trampolining
on concrete terracing, out of my brain.
A falsetto flush was a small price to pay.

Hugging total strangers – no shame!
Every sodden Saturday, dreary floodlit evening
game forgotten. Our little pick 'n' shovels
had turned the earth around,
for every mousey sound, cheers ring.

5.   Sealed in dust

One of those shops to browse never buy,
out from the rack of featureless bargains
he pops, suited like the rows themselves.
At first, I don't fix him at all,
then the 'moush' clicks countless games:
'Do you still go down?'

As much a fixture as Captain Morgan Rum
on Bob Bank roof, redbrick outdoor bogs
all gone like him with Michael Foot
donkey-jacket, for years my talisman
even when we were for the drop;
for years a passing conversation –
'Promotion! I feel it in my waters!'
I recall his prophetic sign.

Never knew his name, the programme-seller
who changed his coat after decades
to a bright, luminous yellow,
who always had a quip
ready as change: stood
when Portsmouth took the Grange,
when Man U. caused havoc,
when Chelsea did the pincer movement.

'Yeah, what about yourself?'
'No way! The Top Man done for me!'
I shake my head in disgust, amongst
the odd-sized trousers nobody wants
in a Bay that could be Liverpool, Swansea.
In a cupboard, untouched, my programmes sealed in dust.

6. Derby day

St Mary's Street Monday night
all quiet on the derby front
till, sudden as smashing glass,
the yellow-sharded police
pierce the scene –

                        my window gaze
became a TV operation.

The two fawn limousines
branded 'Swansea Hire' were ambushed,
occupants drained of liquid,
most in uniform of Burberry caps
and fawn jackets to match
the bodywork,
                              fingers pointing
up-yours at insults tossed.
Searched in doorways, ogled
by a parade of electric guitars,
rummaged for tools of the trade.

Dragged into waiting wagons,
for doing nothing,
                              except Intelligence
of a trashing. They'd planted
their flags of feet –
                              limos empty
as their victory seemed.

7.   Latterday Friday

Leon Jeanne! As though we'd signed
some exotic foreigner, from Marseilles maybe:
second name pronounced 'Gee-anne!'
with an exclamation mark tagged on.

Not this *Lan-rum-knee* boy, 19,
two kids, dubbed junkie and alkie,
a latterday Robin Friday
without the opportunities.

v. Swansea I saw him perform,
certainly a Friday, more trickery
than Uri Geller, bending the opposition
with willpower of both feet.

He'd come through it, I thought,
Chairman Sam's own prodigy:
dried and starched in a clinic,
they'd smoothed his ragged skin.

Now, needle-point in the ball,
the needle to his head,
blown up too inflated:
every kick a broken bone.

8.   Blue Army, Jack Army

Cardiff 1 – Swansea 0

The flags contradict each other:
Union Jacks, dragons, Ulster
under whose red-handed sail
they rise and fall in waves.

A single stand of sea-creatures
who tentacle together, even swim
breast-stroke to rhythmic taunting,
jeering a minute's mourning.

Neighbours, divided by high fencing,
our slum-gypo goading
and the hiss of a gas-a-Jack
retched up to match their attack.

'Blue Army! Blue Army!' drumdown seats,
our team in ironical green.
Winning goal to force faces under,
we mock as they go down.

9. Under the bridges

Cardiff 0 – Stoke 1

Before the match, dangerous celebrations,
every street spilled cans, kicked spinning.

Drunk on expectations, talk flying.
Wings flagging five minutes from time!

We dropped like shot pigeons:
under the bridges, white-grey spatters.

No echoes under those chant-arches:
our silence was fuming.

Treading on pavements of glass,
we buried our heroes with blame.

For our blue tribe another season,
other times in sun, in rain.

10. Until the team

Cardiff City 1 – QPR 0

Until the team come on
there are scenes of dream in camera
of 'Where do all these people come from?'
and, imposed on all that show of blue,
the absurd St David's emblem
we'd thought was the flag of another nation.

I buy a banner to wave in sway,
but carry it like an umbrella
anticipating the chants like rain,
especially 'Men of Harlech'
whose words go 'Duh d' duh, d' da da!'
We're distant, as giant balls are rolled
by the engineers of the occasion.

Until the team come on
and our voices are lost in belonging:
minutes from time, when we finally score
our 'Yeah!' screams soar
like a release after 30 years
down in the Dungeon,
hugging my son who I used to raise
like a trophy at a rare celebration.
Our whistleblown tears of elation.

11. In the close season

A poet without paper and pen.
An artist without paint or pencil.
A cockerel without a hen.
A mole without a hill.
A television without electricity.
A twitcher without binoculars.
A song without a melody.
A night sky without stars.
A guitar without strings.
A scientist without reason.
A bird with clipped wings.
A fan in the close season.

Rebel voices

1. Songs in my head

for Andrew Bartz

There are no better tickets
than these gifts you give
these rattling boxes
passed like illicit substances
at our occasional booze-ups.

I want to praise now
long before any elegy
your studiously penned
funny and angry titles:
THIS TAPE KILLS 99%
OF ALL FASCISTS DEAD
of the NOT WHAT IT READS one:
you should've had a band
just for the covers alone.

Journeys unwind: the brown path,
the shining rails, the thin
road leading away
to Africa or Ireland
obscure names like places
only you discover,
Marxman, Best Shot, Tarika:
villages into towns into countries.

The music of your recordings
the passports never stamped
the borders always open:
songs in my head flying.

2. Talk about talk!

for Alun Roberts

Talk? You could persuade
the sheep up Asda's
to stop pestering shoppers
as they load their cars!
You'd outjabber the Rev. Paisley
and Ian Paisley Junior,
you could chatter for Wales
at every distance, hurdling
Labour donkey devotees
in the process, pole-vaulting Tories
with your spiked views.

Talk about talk! You'd outgossip
the tallest columns
of the most scurrilous papers,
you'd interview journalists
who'd come for a story,
a one-man street-meeting
(no need for a megaphone)
you'd banter with young and old,
burble to babies, teeter at toddlers
non-stop, if aliens landed
you'd probably coax them
into forming a Socialist Republic of Jupiter!

No full-stops only the odd comma
for your inhaler, between fags,
your enthusiasm burning holes
and filling them with tomorrows.

3. Through black rain

for Tim Richards

If, on a wet Thursday evening
in the middle of a dark December
at a dead-end valley institute
(due to be closed down)
you came to talk to a meeting
and only two turned up
(one of them the caretaker!) –
you'd still speak with summit passion,
you'd still leave with optimism
not needing 10 pints of whoosh
to believe in that revolutionary
change from without and within.

We're brothers of these notions
yet we joke about campaigns:
buckets of lime and pasted posters,
Che Guevaras on traffic islands,
police in courts to sit you down
and MP's surgeries with no prescriptions.

Towards the mountain, your many talents
are paths and each direction
brings a challenge: arrêtes
and chasms. You'd never follow,
you'd be armed with a torch
deaf to thunder, knowing
we'd climb through black rain
to breathe clear for the first time,
at the top your memorial inscribed
THE STRUGGLE HAS JUST BEGUN.

Here, Now

Here, now, in this our Cymru
they come for him,
my friend and comrade Tim,
like Joseph Coffin's henchmen
from the debtors' court
taking the beds from under them.

Here, now, in this our Cymru
they connived to put
the fear of the State,
to copper-quake his family,
they want to threaten us all:
'Keep quiet, or you will break!'

Not Iraq, the Taliban or Zimbabwe,
but here, now in this our Cymru,
dawn raid like the Six Counties,
dragged over the mountain to Ponty,
my friend and comrade Tim.

Here, now, in this our Cymru,
they can listen in but never hear
our internetting solidarity;
they can spy with binocular eyes,
yet never see the text within
ourselves and friend and comrade Tim.

The safest asylum

(Jenny Marx in London)

'We believe that Englishmen are interested in anything by which the old-established reputation of England, as the safest asylum for refugees of all parties and all countries, may be more or less affected.' (Marx & Engels, letter to the Spectator, *June, 1850)*

So many countries we're fugitives from, my Liebchen,
each one where you adopted a different name:
now you are Mr Charles here in England,
in this place of the safest asylum.

But what will become of us, I plead,
Fawksey bites my breasts, they bleed.
I have seen Destitution on the stern face
of the landlord, its plagues of disgrace.

I have heard Starvation pounding
with the sound of bailiffs hounding
us out of this Chelsea street,
stealing the ground from under our feet.

We've pawned every family jewel,
we've even sold the baby's cradle,
we barely exist on floorboards now:
destiny cannot feed our mouths.

Where is Friedrich with his cotton gins,
or Uncle Philips with his electric machines?
My family spurns me as a criminal,
thoughts of the workhouse are so vile.

Liebchen, you believe something will turn up,
yet there is only water in our cup
and for all my faith in your mind's bed,
there's no sleep as my milk runs red.

Putting the past in the dock

The politician harangued the propagandists,
publicly exposing his righteousness.

The Premier footballer dropped his fortune
into the busker's grounded hat.

The solicitor gave his time for free,
without a pound-ticking talking clock.

The popsinger took his ego for a walk
in the woods and lost it on purpose.

The General insisted on negotiations,
putting his past in the dock.

The model welcomed droops and wrinkles,
friends who spoke candidly of death.

The estate agent admitted the best roof
was made of stars and walls of bush.

The City trader denounced all shares
as guns not ploughs; stocks for torture.

The accountant shifted all that money
onto a Pacific island that was disappearing.

The examiner only asked one question –
'What is the meaning of Zen?'

Stress management

Acupressure not acupuncture.
DIY. Same results. Sort of.
Preferably with colleague of same sex,
avoids complications, distractions,
takes up less marking time.
Apply hands-on to the head,
can be done breaktimes
but not when driving.
Backache the biggest one,
statistically proven. Two finger technique.
Oooh, nice one doctor!
Sitting up not lying down.
Exercise more often. Daily walk.
Get a dog, but don't let it
loose on your exam papers.
Inspection. The Big One.
Eat more fruit. Avoid soya and beans,
you'll be woken by night-flatulence,
sleep deprivation a form of torture.
Imagine you're on a journey
preferably train (it'll be delayed),
you'll discard your baggages
out the window one by one
your worries, count them.
Above all, learn how to breathe:
inhale without meaning,
exhale your perfect vision,
words, song, sexual position.
Don't, whatever you do, don't
listen to where the stress takes you.
It's a conman, a quack doctor
when it insists 'Leave, get away!
You could be doing something useful

like picking up leaves from the line,
or embarking on a real train journey
to somewhere north of beyond . . . '
Manage it, manage it as though
it was the only one under you.
Manage as we do you. Tell it
where to go, what to do.

Permission to kill

When I'm eighty-four
and bound to a chair all day,
an adult nappy wrapped
around incontinent parts nightly –
you have permission to kill me.

When I'm eighty-four
and can't drink wine and beer
because of the side-effects of medication,
can't read because glaucoma's got me –
you can joyfully poison my water.

When I'm eighty-four
and my legs are elephantine,
my joints are racks of pain,
my meals are on prescription –
lay me in a boat on Cardigan Bay.

When I'm eighty-four
and the stairs are like Pen-y-fan,
our house like Cardiff prison,
my mind a dried-up reservoir –
drive over me in our car.

When I'm eighty-four
find me an atheist religion
ensuring ghosthood and time-travel
and I promise not to waste it like Faustus –
be a modest spirit, respect sun and moon.

Every orchestra

Every orchestra needs the viola,
between the trilling and the flow,
so seldom to be given solo,
like altos in the choir.

Every team needs the grafter
the player who holds,
getting dirty with tackles:
unsung beginner of the goal.

Every band needs the bass-player,
never the primadonna,
in time with the song
like the beat of imagination.

Every magazine needs the stamper,
the eye-for-detail subber,
the one whose name appears
between the lines of others.

Every school needs the caretaker,
the seats and tables shifter,
who runs the heat in winter,
making veins from the corridors.

Every family needs the listener,
two in the morning phone-keeper:
the ever-ready ear
to prompt and reassure.

Every orchestra needs the viola,
rarely the melody, the holder
of arch between eye and eye:
the hollow of vibrating air.

The pig . . . (in) there

(Thanks to Robert Wyatt)

Flat concrete sky,
disused legs,
metallic straitjacket,
striplight suns in rows:
no clouds.

Fed to time,
no searching with nose,
not even dreams
of mud and trees,
truffles a luxury
outside, foreign.

Ground does not give
to her fleshy form,
young suckle tugging
her bloated dugs.
Space is an inch
to bristle and twitch.

Soon they're taken,
stolen orphans
to be fattened,
scrying like infants
abandoned at nursery
for the first time,
their absence felt
like limbs lopped off.

She'll be fit for the chop,
the humane electrodes
will bring convulsions,
the quick knife
to the throat, her blood
will run as she could not.

The Cale variations

Between Mynydd Du and *y pwll glo*,
on the edge of limestone escarpments
and waterfalls of consonants;
between your father and mother
and the tongues of underground rivers.

A *Sons and Lovers* upbringing:
leather belt meant to harden,
though not the drunken targeting.
Music your destination:
the strict time of lessons
and practising, the chapel organ
where you found early fame.

In your teens, another organ
graced the chapel, deflowering
the minister's virgin daughter,
the blasphemy of spilt blood
as Christ impassively looked on.

Viola your chosen one:
velvet-petalled flower,
not winding pansy stems
of the ubiquitous violin,
nor the fiery geranium
of the cello's range.

You took her, Viola
and made her your own.
Took her flying over oceans,
while the piano's chords and arpeggios
were river, lake and shore
always tugging you home.

Away from mountain, pit
and cave of chapel walls
with their Biblical print,
you learnt to unlearn,
turned instruments inside out,
taught the music of silence
and revolution of scores
which resembled hieroglyph.

You had to go far to return:
Cordoba, Casablanca and Amsterdam,
the envoy with nobody listening,
till back to Swansea eventually
with the sea and Dylan
looming, booming intonations.

You dammed the river
when you elbow-punched
the piano keys, it was a burial
of all those stuffed suits,
trussed and ready for carving.
Shock was the treatment
you gave as Copland flirted,
but you were a letter away
from Cage with his joke
on the blank surfaces of art.

The Big Apple a windfall
you picked up, ran away with,
ate with gusto. Except
it was drawn in plastic
by Warhol, in a factory
with open doors to courtesans
of the night-street after beat.
Blood-brother with Reed
of knife-sharp needle-point,
you rose with scrapers
to fall down the shaft.

It took years for you
to cover the tracks,
still engrained tributaries
of coal on the hands.
Years when you became
a sailor of the *grand*
lifting a lid to catch the wind;
a poet of the riverbank
close-watching debris tangle
with bright, resilient plants;
a follower of ghosts
along galleries of history;
a balladeer in village pub
calling lost friends from dark;
a lone accompanist to films
shown in a derelict theatre;
a swimmer with a lamp
in the streams which disappear.

You have returned from exile
without coming back.
The chapel organ's an avalanche
of collapsing roofs, the piano-strings
echo as we search for you
in those uncharted caverns.

(With thanks and acknowledgement to John Cale's autobiography 'What's Welsh for Zen' and, above all else, his songs, poems and music from the Velvet Underground to today, some of whose titles I've referred to in this poem.)

All they want from you

(for Richey, wherever he may be)

They won't find you there:
the divers for clues
the beachcombing detectives
cameramen awaiting a catch.

There's nothing wrong with crossing
as long as you come back,
the high tide takes away
cargo lighter than coal.

And I've found you where
I least expected in the ease
of a room, images beyond despair,
your rhythms spanning the gloom.

The headlights career onwards,
the tolling a clash of coins,
but there is something moving
below the wires' strain.

Seeking Victor Jara

One day I will go
one day I will go to Chile.

I'll learn how to say it the Spanish way
and I'll visit the Estadio Chile
to watch a football game,
the sport that means so much to me.

I'll feel the passion rising up
like the condor above the Andes,
sense the music of a passing movement,
a crescendo towards the net.

One day I will go to Chile
and join with the thousands
who fill the terraces with growing,
the colours of nations
worn without any warring.

Remember how his songs were stopped –
his splintered hands, the strings
made into kidnap knots
and how the case became a coffin,
the chamber of vibrations
a morgue where he was thrown.

One day I will go to Chile
and learn how to say his name
in the cheer with a score,
every stretching neck his finger-board.

The tree & the tower

There's a wide spread of petticoat
August auburn on the outside,
green facing in, where we hide
in that *sensuality of the shade*
Yeats marked so delicately.

The first to initial that smooth
parchment of the copper beech.
Augusta Gregory in autumn
widowed in buffed red-brown:
WBY losing its clarity to time.

Weathering and the admiring palms
have rubbed so many autographs,
obscuring Hyde, *An Craoibhinn Aoibhinn*
his Gaelic name of the knife
and others queried or forgotten.

The tower remains, its gyring stairs
up to the stars, the ghosts of Normans
who built to oversee, while Coole
has long been left to fester down,
for uneasy spirits we're waiting on.

Over the tower's roof a sword in the east,
under the leafy dome we trace
a constellation of friends made myth;
under the bridge blown in rebellion
the stream translates script-reflections.

Notes: The title refers to The Autograph Tree in Coole Park and Yeats'
house at Thoor Ballylee. Yeats' friend, author and translator Douglas
Hyde, signed his name as ACA on the tree, i.e. Gaelic for 'the most
beautiful branch'.

Sundial, Coole Park

We stand in the August box
myself and Niamh, bee-child
she'll be off in a jitter,
sniffing flowers into the distance.

Together we make two shadows,
the sun lowing at our backs
we are two arms of the time
precise enough past five o'clock.

Her brambly hair, my mossy head:
for a beam I'm the hour
and she's the minute,
charcoaled yet not burnt.

I should be content to demonstrate
the brass dial, to commune
with Yeats and his ilk
who stood at Coole in sun-tide.

But there are hedges tempting
as a house made of sweets,
there are people in wolves' clothing,
giant trees there for the climbing.

And so, I chase her winging shadow
across the waxy surface of lawns,
as Yeats those faery visions,
the lost children, the disappearing lake.

Rizla poems

Rizla poems in Gaelic:
the tissue as fine
as a layer of skin.
The smallest script
I've ever seen,
inside the briefed envelope,
so light and sudden
they must've been smuggled in
with a roll of the palm.

The words in intricate lines
telling of how long, of journeys
and of children, their silent
letters pausing often,
afraid of detection.

These poems are litmus
to the sweat I can't
stop coming, so I'll grain
their delicate chain to my hands:
it'll link me to those men,
begin to translate their pain.

Gaelic on Inis Mór

Beyond the litter bins, road signs,
grants given and shop names –
as you cross the water
it shimmers the air
from till to till
in the grasping supermarket,
from pony-cart to pony-cart
as horsemen banter,
from father to sons
who dive into the harbour.

The waves rise with it,
tides turn on tongues
which have been born
into its many ways of being;
it has been reclaimed
from landscapes of stone,
boulders lifted and laid
into walls, netting the soil.

The wild goats stare it
in the face, their thistly beards
and four wise looks
at the edge of an outcrop
and yet not wavering.
It survives as donkeys die
with too heavy a burden
and tourists eagerly try
to reel up the roads
to process, label, claim.

There are cliffs on the island
no man has ever seen,
but if you gaze long enough
the rocks will become seals basking,
seals transform to maighdean mara
and their shapes are mouths
lipping the name *Mór*.

Note: Inis Mór – the largest of the Aran Islands, off the coast of co. Galway (maighdean mara – mermaid).

Chaplin in Waterville

Charlie Chaplin stands on the promenade
facing the wrong way, towards the town.
He should be tracking the weathers
as they turn in a single day:
squalls, sea-breezes, clouds like turfsmoke.

Instead, he clown-lips towards
the internet café, the cables
which ring the world from this Ring
of Kerry, the accents gathered
from all the compass points.

Chaplin totally still, no penguin walk,
no windmilling walking-stick:
going green and seasick
in his coppery state, as if
tides trawled under his boots.

Between languid lough and spirited sea,
between the tidal estuary revealing
its soft vowel-shapes of sand-banks
and the craggy consonants of cliffs,
still stealing every photo opportunity.

In the climate of cars

In the climate of cars
the wind is the keening
of the flood-refugees:
sand-bags form parapets
soon breached, possessions
are turned to mulch.

In the climate of cars
the headlights pierce
like insurer's eyes
and print's always smaller
than you can decipher.
The lowlands become estuaries,
whole species are shifting
northwards, we cannot cope
with their venom, mosquitoes
thrive on the lake-fields.

In the climate of cars
we declare war on the elements,
but we are losing:
water and its high battalions
no army can conquer.
Soon we'll make for the mountains
in our millions, forgetting
they were once below the sea.

Safe

Down at the bus-station late night
someone's screaming it's like
the ward of a mental hospital
before the pill-trolley, he volleys
a strangled wail down plastic tubes
of shelters. I stare ahead
New York subway survival kit,
till out of a shop doorway
a no. 1 hairchop girl hops
in front like she lived
in a burrow down sewers
'Fiver for-a burger an-a cuppa?'
hardly older than my daughter
but eyes ringed metallic –
two steps more a boy appears
squeezing out of a pavement crack
stepping around and sparring
'Only a coupla quid! C'mon man!'
My two coins are it's 'Safe!'
and they're gone, not a breath
of booze or a mad grin, just two kids
and that word stammering
across every sleeper home –
safe as houses, money in the safe,
safe with them, no waste,
my meagre gift, their cups
cradled and cooing steam.

Fire the house

I will show respect for all you do,
listen and nod and agree with you.
I'll bring you tea and coffee too
not mentioning the lack of one 'Thank you'.

I will shut every door to stop the draught,
boil your potatoes till they're soft,
never sound like an ape when I laugh,
hand to mouth politely when I cough.

I'll even go without the footie on TV,
wipe the toilet seat after a pee,
always try to eat daintily
and, after a few pints, come home early.

I will suppress my farting foible,
never swear at the dinner table,
buy anniversary flowers and grovel,
never argue from my high pedestal.

In short, I'll do just as you please,
anticipating the bedroom tease . . .
you turn your back to sleep in peace
while I fire the house as you freeze.

Nothing as petty

There is nothing as petty as a man
when he can't have what he most desires.
he will not accept that you're tired,
that you want to embrace in comfort,
that, just for once, you long
to take your time instead
of the ever-quick in-out-in-out.

There's nothing as childish as him
beating his head down on the pillow
like some spoilt child denied
another sweet, another toy, another comic.
And how he's so determined
to prevent your sleep after this,
he turns from lover to torturer in a minute.

There's nothing as ill-tempered as him
pacing the night below our room,
when all you require is rest,
is somebody to willingly listen,
is a hug to warm a winter's night,
is sleep's solace slipping down deep.

There's nothing more moody than a man
who thinks he can be lead by his passion,
his hands trying to climb up your back
like two scaly insects you'd slam
till they were dead and throw
out the door onto the mud:
his body's hard shell at the rejection.

Scream the days

'Once again the diamond stylus of imagination skips uncontrollably across the scratched vinyl of metaphor.' – Chris Meredith (*'Sidereal Time'*)

1. Afternoons keep returning

Afternoons are crazy,
I can't round them up
(I'm a hopeless collie) –
they must be on speed
(wish they'd take wacky backy) –
they refuse to sit down.
All my yells and spittle
won't shift them –
they're a Committee of Fooldom
smiling like a goat a-hanging.
I'm lost trying to tell them,
they listen to the rain
drumming its fingers incessantly
on tables, paper drizzles
back and fore.

When I get home tears
the size of schools of fish
swim into my eyes,
wasp-nest bags below them,
ears a worry of gnats,
my mouth a crater
where they swirl and burn.

Afternoons keep returning
to tease and taunt.
No amount of grids
can pen them –
their canvas a boxing-ring.

2. Banish Tuesdays

I'd banish Tuesdays
but not to Mantua
where they'd write letters back
in their succulent prose:
further than Brecon even
to places beyond
our grand new road-signs.
Let them wander the hills
aimlessly ashamed,
days with lost identity
becoming Shoesdays,
Snoozedays, Bluesdays.

Tuesdays give me insomnia:
I awake panic-sweating.
The bars of their time-table
tattoo my eye-balls,
I dread their needles
scraped across my retina,
they grow in my stomach
like an ulcer,
their many mocking heads
all rock, their teeth grip
and I'm shaken.
I've seen a lion
treat a man like this.

I'll not succumb to their madness.

3. The scream has come

The boy with the Munch mask
is staring into my room
through the door's wired-up glass.
The Scream has come here.

Amphetamania begins to wane,
as later his drooping head
falls to the desk,
his ears are buzzing
because someone's slapped
his parody of the painting.
His hair's snipped
as he dozes through work.

With home-time beckoning
he's awake to the possibilities
of evening, of TDA
where CCTV can't reach him,
he breaks a pair of scissors
in half, using the sharper blade
to stab, he flaps to the window
like a bird trapped
in a building, his hat's a bandage
and the Scream's stashed
next to his heart:
shocks silent its beating.

4. Cut-ups

The boy in the corner
notched, as ever, between window and heater
skull-faced and smokey pallor,
wielding his lethal scissors
with the skills of a tailor.

He's slicing avidly through 'Bliss'
and 'She', 'Just 17' and 'Miss',
selecting the girls with a hiss
of the blades, lips he'll never kiss:
he refuses to hold a pen like this.

I see them gathered and spread:
the pair of long legs,
eyes gouged out, an amputated head
and bulbous breasts, to the bed
of white paper his lusts are glued.

5. Friday's stalk

Fridays creep up with a knife.
They're out on Community Care
but should be locked away.
They should be heavily sedated –
there's no trip-switch
to stop them shorting the circuit.
They stalk with loose wires
hanging in the damp.

A menace to relaxation
they spy pieces of dirt
in corners of your head never hoovered.
Fridays will electrocute
even the most earthed person
in a bath of liquor no protection
from the grin of plastic coating
the deadly charge within.

6. Led by the sun

There are days I feel like whistling
to the blackbird on our fence,
I feel like singing some vague
inarticulate song of longing,
when mist rises in late afternoon
and we climb to our home
in the purpley-pink-yellow,
in clouds like whispers
of promises not yet sown.
Days of daffodil scent strong
as seduction, so sensual
and yet so common,
days I'm led by the sun
which leaps over the horizon
springing down to the river,
skinny-dipping there in all
its re-born vigour.

Note: TDA – Take and Drive Away